来自中国的
明信片

POSTCARDS
FROM
CHINA

INGRID BOOZ MOREJOHN

SERINDIA CONTEMPORARY

THE CHINA COUNTDOWN

In July of 2006 I moved with my family from Sweden to Chengdu, capital of Sichuan Province in Southwest China. I had been working in China, off and on, since 1985 when I first travelled there on the Trans-Siberian Railway. But apart from a few years spent in Hong Kong in the late 1980s, I had never lived in China, only travelled around, visiting every province as a photographer, writer and tour guide. During these years Sichuan Province held a special fascination for me and when the opportunity came to move to China, Chengdu was the logical choice. One year quickly turned into many and we found ourselves rooted and at home in this multimillion resident city situated at the bottom of a cloudy basin surrounded by the mountains of Tibet to the West and China Proper to the East.

Every Chinese person knows that Chengdu has its own special flavor and atmosphere, accented by its fiery cuisine, ever present overcast weather and a reputation as home to pandas, poets, politicians and teahouses. My 1985 Sichuan memories of drinking endless cups of tea and munching watermelon seeds whilst sitting on creaky bamboo chairs in small teahouses returned powerfully when I travelled back, but this former Chengdu slowly vanished during our years there. We witnessed Chengdu modernize and develop, still retaining its wonderful laid back atmosphere but becoming more and more cosmopolitan, "modern" and, sadly, heavily polluted.

I relished the grittiness, the amazing life and pulse that is everyday China. Our first four years were in the Tibetan quarter of Chengdu, near Wu Hou Temple; the last four in the affluent Tongzilin area. Rarely did a day pass without us seeing something in the street that amazed, delighted, enchanted, disgusted or appalled. China is a continuous circus of shows, the greatest show on earth.

After eight years it was time to move on. To somehow capture my deep feeling for Chengdu and its wonderful residents, I decided to take a photograph each day of my last 100 days and post each one with a short text on my Instagram feed, hoping that my followers would share my last days "as they slipped away." After spending almost 30 years rummaging around China, I had a clear idea of what I wanted to show in these digital postcards, and I avidly went in pursuit of my "shot list" of everyday scenes. Street photography is easy in China; life just happens all over the place all the time. Smartphone photography has also evolved to a higher level of quality, making it easy for me to always have a ready but nonthreatening camera at hand.

The relaxed nature of the local Sichuanese people became the lead player in my #chinacountdown, and every day was filled with fun in pursuit of another image.

During the countdown my Instagram followers increased, mostly with homesick Sichuanese residing in other parts of the globe, their comments of how I had captured something so typical and so true reassuring me that I wasn't stepping on anyone's cultural toes other than with affection and mutual delight. If I missed a day (rarely!), I received admonishments and encouragements to keep the images coming. I never left home without my phone-camera in hand, ready to capture an image out a taxi or bus window or on the street or in a store. I walked countless kilometers in pursuit of my images, but also with the intent to soak up as much of China as I could.

The people I encountered on these peregrinations around the city never hesitated or stopped me from taking their picture, and gladly and openly shared their lives with me, patiently answering my questions and graciously posing for a picture. To them I dedicate this little book.

#thankyou

Ingrid Booz Morejohn
March 2015

DAY 100 The Beginning

Well, peeps, this is the beginning of my China swan song. I'm leaving and there are 100 days to go. I'm going to try to post a picture every day, of the most common things that I see all around me. China Unfiltered in a way, but filtered through my eyes and heart and, like here behind the driver in a motorized rickshaw, the wonderful grime that is China Everyday. I love you China. You are so crazy.

PS. The advertisement here is for a fishing camp outside of Chengdu. Call 'em.

DAY 99 Arboreal Intravenous Drips

Only in China do trees get their own IV drips (in addition to support props). I have never seen this anywhere else. The IV bag is full of medicine and nutrients, and the needles are stuck right into the trunk. With the heavy pollution here, perhaps we should all walk around like this.

DAY 98 China Has Real Fashion Guts

China is the most amazing country for people watching. Women and men alike compose their visual selves with wonderful abandon, imagination and verve. Mixing patterns, textures, materials and styles with a bold palette and a devil-may-care *joie de vivre,* they create fashions that you won't see anywhere else. Famous name brands are boldly copied, imitated or stolen outright. Age is no restriction to skirt hems or wild hairdos. The universal black hair is dyed brown, red, blond or why not blue? Nails are extended, painted or blinged. Contact lenses enlarge irises to imitate large doll eyes, making it an eerie event when gazing into them. Shoes are every shape or design and there seems to be no end to how they can be changed or reshaped. Comfort is definitely not foremost in people's minds, as some of the clothing seems absolutely excruciating to wear — teetering high heels and skintight skirts. As with their western counterparts, a large part of a young single woman's income goes to clothing or handbag purchases. It's only after they begin to think of having children that they finally start putting money away in the bank.

DAY 97 Amazingly Tasteless Lamps and Lighting Fixtures

When China went middle-class, their design sense went out the window. China became a bastion of nouveau-riche tackiness of epic Las Vegan proportions. Oversized lamps in the shape of Cupid's bow and arrows, or here — butterflies — framed by multiple drop-ceilings overwhelm ordinary cement apartments. The Versailles-like overuse of gold and ornamental curlicues would make Marie Antoinette feel right at home. It is actually quite terrifying to sleep under a huge ceiling lamp like this — it might come down any minute. And of course the electrical wiring is so faulty that half the bulbs are usually blown out. The lamps do beat the single 5-watt naked bulb of the 1980s though.

DAY 96 Construction Sites

China is one big building zone, no matter where you go. And everything happens very quickly. You leave for a month and your favorite restaurant is gone and something new has taken its place. The people who worked there are also gone, another relationship severed. Holes are dug and cement is poured. Cranes everywhere. The amount of iron, steel, cement and glass that is consumed by this country has never been matched by any other in human history. This also means building dust and toxic carcinogens in the air, another major contributor to the daily high pollution ratings. My place of work is surrounded by three major highways and several construction sites. Only a decade ago this was countryside mixed with small low-lying buildings and businesses. The constant change makes for a kind of subconscious stress and impermanence, but also excitement, hope and stimulation.

DAY 95 Fighting Corruption

Anti-corruption poster the size of a billboard. "Say no to red packets! Say no to bribery! Being greedy will only lead you to corruption!" The new government is all about cracking down on corruption. One friend who works for a large liquor company says that booze sales are down 30 percent — disastrous for companies that rely on sales that are tied to conspicuous consumption and "gift-giving." Other Chinese friends say that the campaign is pure window dressing. Another side of life in China — corruption — which before was kept more secret but now is so evident, cannot be ignored.

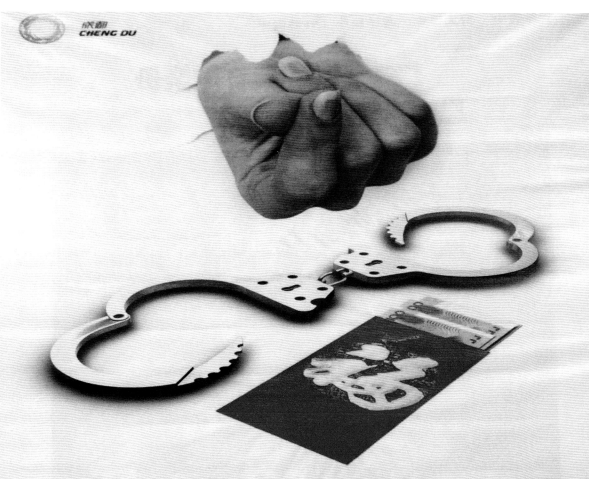

反腐倡廉

拒绝贿赂！ 拒绝红包！
贪心是走向犯罪的第一步！

举报贪腐行为请登录廉洁成都网站：http://www.ljcd.gov.cn/

DAY 94 Sichuan Hotpot

Oh my goodness, the love we have for Sichuan food, it is truly China's greatest regional cuisine. The number of flavors experienced in one mouthful is legendary. Chili hot, Sichuan pepper numbing, sweet, sour, salty, meaty and hearty, it is truly amazing. The humid misty air of the Sichuan basin captures and holds the *mala* (hot and numbing) molecules of all the cooking that is constantly going on. The special numbing, slightly lemony, licorice flavor of Sichuan pepper is not everyone's cup of tea, but once hooked it is difficult not to believe it is among the most enticing taste sensations on earth. The hotpot shown here — to enjoy with several friends — is in a *yuanyang* pot (Mandarin Duck pot) with one side red-hot chilies and the other a red tomato broth. Numerous dishes, both meat and veggie, are ordered and cooked in your broth of choice. Hardy souls prefer the chili side and wimps stay on the red bouillon side. Icy cold beer is a good chaser. Heaven.

DAY 93 Chengdu's Largest Spice Market

To go along with the hotpot, this picture demonstrates how serious we are about chilies in Sichuan. This man is hauling bags of peppers traded from several parts of China. *Wukuaishi* (Five Pieces of Stone) is a massive wholesale spice market selling everything from chilies to cloves, cinnamon bark, mace, ginger, dried algae, fermented bamboo shoots, shiitake mushroom, fermented soy beans, and on and on. An all-pervading heavenly smell of Sichuan pepper hangs in the air. The color red dominates inside the warehouses and the traders are jolly and generous with their laughter, playing mahjong, elephant chess and cards to pass the time. Down the street is the wholesale market for sex toys — but I'll save those pictures for another post!

DAY 92 People Doing Silly Things in Public

I love it when adults do things like this, shouting into their phones at the same time. They don't care that you are taking a picture, and they smile at you at the same time. Sichuanese are wonderfully laid-back people, very forgiving of nosy parker foreigners and - like most Chinese - forced to live and accustomed to living their lives in public. China without the Chinese would be a very sad country indeed. The sheer mass of humanity is overwhelming and often suffocating, but my goodness I am fond of you!

DAY 91 Gnarly Electric Wire Tangles

Does it really have to look like this? Most of the wires here are not used, but once they become obsolete they are cut but NOT removed. Thus the tangle just gets bigger and bigger until sometimes the weight brings down the whole damn contraption. Makes for cool graphic photos though.

DAY 90 People Sleeping in Public Places

It is common to see fully respectable, non-homeless people openly catching some Zs in China. If you have some time left over and you aren't yakking with friends on your cellphone, chances are you're sleeping. Ride a bus and everyone falls asleep like babies within a few minutes. China used to have the very civilized custom of taking a siesta of several hours in the middle of the day. If you visited an office or store, most of the staff was out cold lying on top of their desks or countertops. Many government institutions, like schools, still do this today. The couple here has a legitimate excuse; they are outside the train station waiting for its departure. This method of physically intertwining and supporting each other allows both to rest relatively comfortably.

DAY 89 Playing Cards with Friends

If you're not eating, sleeping or talking in China, you're playing some kind of a game, usually elephant chess (Chinese chess), mahjong or, as here, a card game. The most popular card game in Sichuan, and common all over China, bears the tragi-comic name "Beat the Landlord" (*dou di zhu*) — beat as in "denounce" or "struggle against." Several players play: one is the landlord and the others are peasants struggling against him. The name is a historical reference to the post-1949 early communist era when landlords were denounced and sometimes even beaten to death. The card game is played vehemently, with lots of furious slapping down of cards and — despite gambling being illegal in China — bets being laid.

DAY 88 The Recycler

This retired man supplements his income by recycling trash. Here he is carrying four bags filled with plastic containers. He readily stopped and happily offered up this information: "1.70 renminbi a jin, 50 renminbi for the whole lot that I'm carrying." That is equal to US$8, which is a lot of money if collected daily, and this activity is not unusual for a big city like Chengdu. Very little goes to waste in China; almost everything is recycled and made into new products. But here it is all sorted and picked through in the normal mix of garbage, dirty diapers, broken glass, food waste and all. The job is usually done by people from the lower economic echelons of society. It is hard work, but supports a huge number of people in the country as well as taking care of valuable and precious resources.

DAY 87 Pollution

I didn't want to post this, but it is very much a part of the story. The AQI (Air Quality Index) reading this day was 419, listed as "extremely hazardous, affecting all citizens." The moment I stepped outside I had a headache and throughout the day I felt my lungs hurting. I have been living here for 8 years and I have spent large amounts of the past 29 years in China. I am afraid to know what is ticking away inside of my body. This is also the main reason why I can actually find some comfort in leaving — escape from pollution. But what about all the people who can't leave?

DAY 86 The China Squat

Men in business suits do it, women in high heels do it, pooping babies in split pants do it, grannies and old geezers do it. You have to have done it for a long time to know how to squat comfortably (good weight distribution) and you can't be too hefty. The trick is to relax your leg muscles and let the weight spread out to your bottom, and of course have good balance. Toilets in China are usually squatties and if they are not, many public stalls with "Western" commodes have signs forbidding people to squat on top of the seat ring. Squatting: try it out! There are even tutorials as well as hilarious spoofs on YouTube.

DAY 85 Young Pioneers

Young Pioneers (*hong ling jin*), consisting of children between the ages of 6 and 14, are a ubiquitous sight on the streets of China. After age 14, teenagers can join the Communist Youth League and after that they can of course apply for membership in the communist party. This last step is by no means an easy thing, and the majority of Chinese citizens are not party members (though over 85 million of them are). I met these cheery students just as they got out of school, all clustered around a local shop buying candy and treats. My impression is that most students in China at one time or another become Young Pioneers.

The Young Pioneer slogan:
"Be prepared, to struggle for the cause of Communism!"
To which the reply is:
"Always be prepared!"

The Young Pioneers pledge:
"I am a member of the Young Pioneers of China. Under the Flag of the Young Pioneers I promise that: I love the Communist Party of China, the motherland, and the people; I will study well and keep myself fit [lit. exercise well], and to prepare for: contributing my effort to the cause of communism."

DAY 84 Lanzhou Pulled Noodles

Lanzhou Pulled Noodles (*la mian*) at a tiny Muslim restaurant on Xinguang Lu near our apartment. This dish, with thinly sliced peppers and mutton, costs all of US$2. Delicious! The first time I had la mian was in 1985 in Lanzhou, the capital of Gansu Province. The noodles were served with a generous helping of chili sauce and were a real taste revelation in the bland, impoverished food world of 1980s China. For a long time I thought that the *la* meant "spicy," but later I learned that it means "pulled," as in the way they are made by hand right in front of you. The process involves taking a lump of dough and repeatedly stretching it to produce strands of thin, long noodle. It all goes with lighting speed and the way the noodle-maker slaps the noodles down at the end to shake off excess flour is exciting. Thin slices of mutton and finely sliced capsicum along with a little meat broth and a dollop of chili paste make this a simple but hearty meal.

DAY 83 Street Fruit Vendors

Pineapples, mangoes and bananas are the three most popular fruits in China. I first ate Chinese pineapple (*bo luo*) in 1986 in Kunming (Yunnan Province), and it was a taste and visual sensation with its heavy sugary juice and deep yellow color. Being used to nasty old canned Dole pineapple, I had never seen fruit meat this luscious in color. When pineapple season begins in Southern China, the street vendors come out, deftly wielding their special pineapple knives and cutting away all the spiky eyes. One-sixth of a pineapple costs anywhere from 2-3 renminbi (30-50 cents) and is served on a chopstick skewer. Gorgeous to look at, and extremely refreshing as the temperatures rise.

DAY 82 Sichuan Food

All you other China Food Fans, listen up: *chuancai* (Sichuan style) is def the absolute best Chinese regional cuisine — no discussion. No other area of China can pack so many flavors and taste sensations into one bite — hot, spicy, numbing, sweet, sour, salty all in one, dancing around inside your mouth. Truly heaven on earth, and at the top of our list of things we will miss. Now I just have to figure out how to get that Sichuan pepper out of the country.

DAY 81 Little Dogs with Big Attitudes

Sichuan is full of little dogs with sawed off legs, under-bites and big egos. I'm very fond of street dogs in general but prefer the Southeast Asian ones, taller with lovely curved tails and regal heads. These little Sichuanese mutts are low riders, trotting around the streets on jumpy little legs, scoping out their territory with purposeful looks on their faces, rarely pausing to give you the time of day. They usually belong to someone, as most of them are well-fed and healthy. I have no idea what breed combination they are, something like a corgi-Pekingese combo. Dogs in other parts of China don't look like this and I often wonder how this breed became so common in just this region.

DAY 80 Small Services

Almost anything is possible in China if you can pay for it. This man runs a mobile food cart with cold noodles (*liang mian*) and the woman is a hostess in a private club. He drives his cart around calling out his services and she has heard him through the open window. Noodles and money change hands and everyone is happy. I remember a man in Sweden in the 1980s who lived on the second floor of an apartment building. He would drop down a bucket with money to the hotdog man below and pull up the bucket with the food inside. In Chengdu the city government wants these small businesses to disappear from the streets and only wants them where they can be regulated and controlled. Sounds just like modern-day Sweden. But I love these street vendors; they not only bring enormous color and flavor to everyday life but provide a huge number of small services, and usually bring about good interaction between peoples. Right now the cherry and mulberry sellers are walking the streets with their baskets and bamboo pole carriers. I already posted the pineapple sellers. About once every 10 days the knife sharpener sets up shop outside our back gate and the flower sellers are doing a brisk business, as well as the jumbly carts with their needles, combs, barrettes, back scratchers and feather dusters. I don't like big chain stores and malls — in China they are inhuman and noisy, anonymous and identical to anyplace else in the world. These street vendors are a precious, vanishing part of Chinese life.

DAY 79 Four Character Sayings

Having been around for such a long time, the Chinese have a saying for just about any human condition, situation or desire. You name it, they've got it, all encapsulated in (usually) four Chinese characters. These *chengyu* ("set phrases") are a type of traditional Chinese idiomatic expressions that have their roots in classical literature and history. They are not easy to understand if you don't know the context (or the language), but once explained they are full of meaning and cultural flavor. These sayings are often conveyed in visual puns like these horses carrying Money Trees, which I found being sold beside the cash register at the Tan Family Fish Head Hotpot Restaurant. The saying here is *ma shang you qian*, whereby the meaning *ma shang* = on horseback, and *you qian* = there is money. So?! Ma shang commonly means "immediately." If someone yells at you to get going, you answer ma shang! ma shang! In others words, ma shang you qian means "get rich immediately," a central theme in Chinese thinking. 2014 was the Year of the Horse, and Money Trees (*shenxianshu* = heavenly trees) date from the Han Dynasty, yet they had nothing to do with getting rich but were instead pathfinders or carriers of souls to the Other World of Immortality. There are, however, other Money Trees that connect directly to wealth; pictures of people climbing these to shake down coins and gold ingots were common vernacular posters bought during the Chinese New Year to decorate one's home. For anyone not versed in the intricacies of Chinese culture, history or language, these symbols, hidden meanings and visual jokes are unfortunately wasted and largely only enjoyed for their colorful kitschiness or the thought "Oh China is so unfathomable, ha ha." Trying to figure out the rebus of everyday China is part of the fun for me, and after almost 30 years I have only just begun to scrape the surface.

DAY 78 Babies on Hot Wheels

Not so long ago, China had no domestic factory-made prams or strollers. Clever dads, granddads and local craftsmen made them out of scavenged wheels and bamboo or wooden scraps. Some were quite cool, with a double carriage and a play table between the two seats, where twins or two friends could face each other and bang away with their rattles on the play table. Such strollers are rarely seen in cities today. Simple bamboo strollers with plastic wheels can now be bought online, and also high-tech fully modern ones with swivel wheels, etc. Around the 1980s, the type of stroller pictured here became popular in the cities. These are not so robust and can only be used on a paved or flat surface, and they have that classic wrapped plastic tubing that loves (in imitation of rattan) to come unraveled. This little boy was being pushed around by his grandmother, who is the most common babysitter in China, followed by a granddad or (in the cities) a paid nanny. Parents are off working and daycare — if you can afford it — begins at age 2. Some parents send their toddlers to boarding school during the week. In a country of just about 1.4 billion people, you can imagine there are lots of babies!

DAY 77 Baby Carriers

Used by virtually everyone outside the cities (over 600 million people), traditional Chinese baby carriers are practical, comfortable, easy to tie and works of art, especially if worn by one of China's over 50 ethnic groups, who lovingly embroider the back panel of the carrier. Even quite large children can be carried like this, depending on how much weight your back can take. Normally shaped like a T, the top straps are pulled over the carrier's (yes, both men and women carry the baby) shoulders, crisscrossed over the chest and wrapped around under the bottom of the child, then brought forward again and tied around the waist of the carrier. This woman has an extra bottom tie as well to ensure that the child stays in place. I have never seen a light-colored baby carrier in China; they are all usually dark blue, dark red or black, with an embroidered back panel or, as here, with a nice piece of bedding cloth padded for winter or with thinner cloth for summer. Baby carriers and baby strollers are real class dividers in China, visually dividing country folks from city dwellers as clearly as the state of their skin and hands, which reveals whether they are a worker or an urbanite.

DAY 76 Blue and Green Colored Windows

Living in a dirty aquarium. This photograph is oddly beautiful with its lovely renaissance colors, but why oh why the blue- and green-tinted windows?! When China began opening up economically in the 1980s people gained access to money that could be spent on purely aesthetic rather than utilitarian things. First came the idea that every building surface should be covered in white or pink lavatory tiles (idea: hide bare cement walls). Then the blue- and green-tinted glass craze came in the 1990s. I'm not really sure of the thinking behind this, but when I moved to Chengdu in 2006 I vowed to accept anything but tinted glass windows, especially in a city that rarely sees the sun. To be sure, the color is stronger on the outside than the inside, but the tinting cuts down light and lends a slightly queasy green quality to anything or anyone inside. I live in a building covered in flesh-pink lavatory tiles but thank goodness I escaped the tinted windows. P.S. Just because this building's run-down look doesn't say anything about the interior — if you own your own apartment, you can do anything you like inside, and even the lowliest hovel outside can be fancy and luxurious inside.

DAY 75 Mahjong

A China exposé wouldn't be complete without mahjong. (Pronounced *májiàng* in Chinese.) My first introduction to mahjong was in the mid-1980s in Hong Kong. It was still much looked down upon in Mainland China, illegal actually, but in Hong Kong the high clack of mahjong tiles being shuffled about was ubiquitous. You could hear it in the backs of restaurants, down dark alleys and through the metal grated doors of apartment buildings. When mahjong became legal again in China it spread like wildfire, and it is now the most popular game alongside cards. Personally, I never play and don't know the rules; it is said to be like rummy. The tiles, however, are beautiful and lovely to hold in the hand, decorated with Chinese characters, circles and symbols: dragons, flowers and the winds. They say mahjong was all the rage in the US in the 1920s, when people held China-themed parties and played an American version of mahjong.

DAY 74 Frozen Statues

In a park, in the garden, among trees, down a lane, in any given quiet spot, you might come upon a man or woman looking like this, frozen in time, hunched over as if overcome by some deep melancholy. Actually these people are mobilizing and balancing their "life energy" — their *qi* — in one of the many forms of qigong practiced in China. After standing still for quite some time, this man "woke up," patted himself all over and began his other morning exercises in the garden of our compound.

DAY 73 Chinglish (Chinese-English)

I have to include at least one of these endearing examples of horrible mistranslations in my Countdown of Things Chinese and Chengdu-ese. I don't venture far from home to find most of my Countdown pictures — this sign is in our garden. I also want to point out that I am probably guilty of numerous verbal gaffs when I speak Chinese, so please forgive. Chinglish is absolutely wonderful, hilarious, heartrending and sometimes downright incomprehensible. At best it is full of poetic concern for the viewer: "Mind the slippery slope, fall gently." At worst it is shocking, as in this item featured on a restaurant menu: "The shrimp fucks the cabbage," which should have been translated as "stir-fried dried shrimp with Chinese cabbage" because the words for "fuck" and "dry" sound alike in Chinese. Most of these errors are due to non-English speakers taking verbatim what they find in a dictionary or on their computer translating software. They are like those silly foreigners with nonsensical Chinese character tattoos. I'll end with one alarming case at a hospital in Chengdu where Obstetrics/Gynecology carried a sign that read "Cunt Inspection." There you have it; do you laugh or cry?

请勿跨越　谨防溺水

Please don't skip over in case drowned

DAY 72 Photo Op Hijacking

Set foot outside your door and head to an area where there are loads of domestic tourists, and you are guaranteed to be commandeered into a group photo as the token exotic foreigner: "Look who we met at the..." This happens to foreigners of every skin and hair color, but the whiter and blonder you are, the more attractive a prize you are considered to be in the photo album sweepstakes. Small children are the biggest catch and this has driven many of our kids to tears, fits and downright spitting-hissing-scratching refusal. The Chinese just cannot understand that children can get tired of posing, smiling and getting their cheeks pinched every time they go outside. These two guys were on a junket with their wives from neighboring Gansu Province and a little bit drunk. They were jolly and Belgian Brian is easygoing, so all took place in good cheer. I always say yes to these photos, as I consider them my karmic payback for the thousands of Chinese who I have subjected to my photographic stalking.

DAY 71 Let's Hang Out and Drink Bubble Tea

Bubble tea, or pearl milk tea (*zhenzhu naicha*), is a tea-based drink invented in Taiwan during the 1980s. It is popular all over China and Asia and consists of thick, very sweet milk mixed with black tea and loaded with big brown chewy tapioca balls — the bubbles or pearls. The "bubble" is an Anglicized word derived from *boba*, meaning "large breasts." I love these balls and am trying to work up the courage to ask for an extra helping or two the next time I buy my tea. It's easy to suck too hard on the straw, though, and have one fly down the wrong pipe in the process. Today's weather was lovely, balmy and sunny and these girls were We-Chatting and hanging out at a cafe called *Xixili* (Sicily) not far from work. One bubble tea here costs US$1, an affordable treat for most Chinese.

DAY 70 Things One Does in Public

Where do I begin explaining the many Chinese Things this picture contains? Teahouses? Sleeping in public? Number of iPhones people own? Chinese police? Hmmm…. Chengdu is famous for its teahouse culture and lovely teahouses, which are truly delightful. This one is in the garden of the Chengdu Academy of Art, located in three converted courtyards next to *Kuan Zhai Xiang Zi* (Broad Narrow Alleys) in the old Manchu Quarters of Chengdu. The couple is drinking one of our local teas, Emei Bamboo Leaf Green. Behind them sits a posse of Chinese police and not-so Secret Police. They are also drinking tea. The man and woman both have iPhones or possibly one of the new smartphones that imitates the look of an iPhone. She is actually not asleep but rather watching a movie on hers. He has definitely passed out — not because he has been waiting a few hours for a VIP to arrive at *Kuan Zhai Xiang Zi*, but because this is what Chinese do in public when they have exhausted all other possibilities of hanging out. Eaten? Check. Talked to friends? Check. Fiddled with phone? Check. Smoked umpteen cigarettes? Check. WeChat? Check. Fruit Ninja? Check. Let's go to sleep.

DAY 69 Funky Cigarette Packages

Chengdu is the Panda Capital of China, so it is appropriate that I pick this cigarette brand to represent China's somewhat eccentric relationship to cigarette branding. The first cool cigarette I noticed in the 1980s was a package of imitation Camels, where the camel was instead a dinosaur hanging out by some palm trees and a pyramid. Awesome. The brand was *Kong Long* (Dinosaur). The packaging was soft and flimsy and the tobacco dry and old. I also love the looks of Golden Monkey, Flying Horse and Mango brands. Panda cigarettes are those of the elite despite their kitschy appearance. Both the tobacco and the price carry a punch, over 80 renminbi (US$13) a pack and so strong that one third of the cigarette is filter. This was Chinese Communist Party leader Deng Xiao Ping's cigarette of choice, and decorative posters of the time featured the politician with a cig in hand (as did those of Mao Zedong, who preferred *Zhonghua* — China — a brand instead). Veritable smokestacks the two of them, both lived to a ripe old age, Deng way into his 90s. Panda Brand is Shanghai- based but the tobacco (like Deng) is from Sichuan. Some China tobacco facts: Smoking in China is rampant, at about 400 million smokers, almost all men. Round figures: about 1.6 TRILLION poison sticks are smoked each year. You can imagine the amount of revenue the state-run tobacco industry gets from the sales. And all the smokers seem to be sitting right next to you. The popularity and scarcity of Panda cigarettes has resulted in a "healthy" black market trade. The Shanghai Tobacco Corporation has repeatedly warned consumers about copycat versions, and each Panda packet contains six anti-counterfeiting measures. Many people who purchase Panda cigarettes are not smokers, but buy them simply to offer to officials as "gifts."

熊猫香烟

Panda

上海烟草集团有限责任公司出品

DAY 68 Three on a Motor Scooter

This is not a specific Chengdu thing per se, more a "traffic laws are rarely enforced in China so let's bend the rules and see how much fun that is!" These are all electric motorbikes, which are cheap (1,500-3,500 rmb; US$250-700), quiet (too quiet — you often don't hear them coming up behind you), clean, light and easy to maintain. They have a battery pack and are usually classified as bikes so you don't need a license to drive them. They are allowed on bike paths and sidewalks and are usually not banned in Chinese inner cities. The most people I have seen on a motor scooter in Chengdu was a family of five, with a baby and a toddler squeezed between the parents and another toddler in a backpack carrier behind the mother. No helmets either. Amazingly stupid - but they were foreigners. My favorite picture here is the three real estate agents on their way to a viewing. Ride 'em cowboys!

DAY 67 Everything Means Something Else

China is like an enormous onion with many layers that are peeled away in one's pursuit of meaning and understanding in a complex land. With each layer that falls away you come closer to enlightenment, but you also understand that the ultimate core will forever be beyond your grasp. Language and symbolism are tightly intertwined, and as in a Medieval painting, objects represented usually have more than one meaning. The connection is sometimes the physical appearance of an object but more often the connection is homophonic; an object is represented because it rhymes with something else. The lotus is particularly rich — the lush flowering head, the fresh seeds as well as the dried seed pod, the way it grows in mud but flowers above water with radiant purity and beauty, all have powerful symbolism. The lotus flower (*lian hua, he hua*) symbolizes marriage. *He* rhymes with "harmony" and "bring together/connect," and *lian* with "uninterrupted" and "united." The seed pod (where seeds represent "many children") is already quite large when the flower starts blooming, which is considered an early sign that the family will have many sons. Not only used as a decorative symbol, the lotus is eaten as a vegetable when cooked and considered a sweet treat when candied. The root and seeds are both eaten and the leaves can be used as food wrapping. The entire plant is a symbol of purity and immutability as it rises from the mud pure and clean.

DAY 66 Filth and Aesthetics

With this picture I am NOT commenting on public spitting and nose-blowing onto the street, small children peeing and pooping directly on the floor, excessive noise levels, blatant smoking directly in front of No Smoking signs, apartment balconies overflowing with garbage, broken furniture and dead plants, filthy public toilets and restaurant floors overflowing with spat-out bones, cigarette butts and miscellaneous detritus. No, I am talking about aesthetics. This picture shows the staircase at a Chengdu restaurant popular among locals and foreigners alike. It serves absolutely amazingly good Sichuan food. We love it. But it is FILTHY. The floor is so greasy that it is hazardous to walk on. The carpet is frayed, original color unrecognizable. The two pots once held plants that have long since died. The plant soil is rock hard and is littered with discarded cigarette butts. The pots are cheap plastic ones and they are breaking apart, small bits littering the floor. The painting was at one time quite nice, a classic landscape scene of pavilions, rockery, magical islands and trees rendered in cork, an art form that is specific to Eastern China. The glass is so filthy that it is hard to see the actual scene, and god help you if you happen to brush up against it or the greasy walls. The long-suffering waitresses run up and down these stairs with huge heavy dishes of their delicious food. I joked last time that the food is so good because the cooks cut off snippets of the frayed, greasy carpet and use them to replenish the cooking stock. A cockroach that was walking along the frame of the painting perked up his antenna when I mentioned this; he probably agreed. Why is there such a total lack of interest in keeping a public place clean?

DAY 65 Pig Slop and Gutter Oil

A truck loaded with restaurant food scraps. This trio has just carried a blue container out of a restaurant, a scene witnessed daily all over China. The waste will be taken to farms in the countryside where it'll be fed to pigs or, much worse, be recycled into what is known as "gutter oil" or "drainage oil." This recycled oil is extracted and refined from food waste like this and is unscrupulously resold to restaurants or more commonly small street vendors who deep-fry cheap snacks like *youtiao* (fried bread sticks). Food production and food safety are major issues in China.

DAY 64 Outdoor Dining

There is nothing chic or cozy-European about Chinese outdoor eating. It's tiny children's-sized stools and low Formica-covered tables placed outside a restaurant with a dirty sidewalk underneath. A plastic container of thin tissues and perhaps a small decanter of soy sauce and one with vinegar. And of course extra chili paste here in Sichuan. But the food is usually excellent and the company of good friends huddled together slurping their noodles or loudly picking through their food is heartwarming. I often envy the Chinese; they are seldom alone, there is always a friend or colleague to call to share a meal with. The food is cheap, the service brisk (sometimes brusque) and it is easy to find a place to eat. The restaurant with the most people eating outside is the one to choose.

DAY 63 Sheer Flesh Tone Stockings

Not sexy. But practical. Men and women alike wear sheer stockings. Black or dark blue for men, flesh-colored for women — even when wearing sandals. The ground is so dirty that people prefer to keep their feet covered. Walking barefoot is virtually unheard of, and a person doing so is usually mentally deranged and homeless. Other than the pope, I had never seen men wear what I considered ladies socks until I first came to China. In the 80s some men's shoes had high heels and metal studs that clicked on the ground when they walked. Poodle perms for men were also the rage as well. Quite disconcerting. The Chinese take good care of their feet, nail clippers are *de rigueur*, a foot bath is a common article in most urban homes, and medicinal foot massages and pedicures are a welcome luxury. China is one of the world's leading sock producers. Indeed, there is a small city in Eastern China's Zhejiang Province that produces over 8 billion pairs of socks a year, a third of the world's production. The town - Datang - is more widely known by its nickname, "Sock City."

DAY 62 Foreign Brand Names in Chinese

There are many ways of translating foreign brand names so that they can be written in Chinese. You can do it phonetically, choosing characters that sound similar to the foreign pronunciation. This usually makes the name longer than necessary and also quite meaningless. You can crunch down the length by using only the first character of each word. An example is Audi - *Ao Di* (Brighten Profoundly). This method is used by almost half of foreign companies. You can translate the real meaning of the brand name if it has a particular meaning, but it won't reconnect back to a globally recognized brand name. An example is Volkswagen - *Dazhong Qiche* (Car for the Masses). One-quarter use this method. A third and risk-free method (where no puns or jokes can be made about your company name) is to think up a completely new name with a meaning that suits your product, for example Pizza Hut - *Bi Sheng Ke* (Certainly Brings Guests). According to marketing polls, choosing a Chinese translation is most successful if you find both a phonetic translation that sounds similar to the original language, and a translation that conveys a meaning connected to the product. The Swedish company IKEA is a good example. Ikea in Chinese is pronounced *Yi Jia (Jia Ju)* and means Pleasant Family (Furniture). It has become a very well-known and highly successful brand name. I have heard that Ikea has had their own unfortunate language mishaps with their Swedish product names that we think nothing of in Swedish, but which had to be changed in English-speaking countries. A few examples: a desk called "Jerker," a water spray can named "Fukta" and the "Fartfull" workbench.

DAY 61 Food Transport

This lady with a newly slaughtered pig wrapped up in plastic bags is on her way to a restaurant or a hole-in-the-wall street market. During wintertime this is not a problem, but in summertime it's another thing altogether. In the market the meat hangs without refrigeration until it is sold, usually by the end of the afternoon. The Han Chinese love pork more than any other meat. China produces and consumes half of the world's hog production.

There are two other cool things with this picture. The ubiquitous red-checkered front and back apron and sleeve protector, and the attached motorcycle handlebar mittens that usually are only used in winter. They are attached to the handlebars and you just slip your hands in and hold on. You don't need gloves and they are very warm.

DAY 60 Rubbernecking

The Chinese are great gawkers. Why not, I say. I love it as well. And there is ALWAYS something to watch in China. Two cars have a fender bender. Forty people gather to see how the drivers are going to hash it out. Someone cracks up on their motorbike and lies bleeding — same thing. A couple having a nasty spat, fisticuffs, is a spectacular opportunity for some free entertainment. Foreigners eating noodles at an outdoor restaurant, not so interesting anymore, but that can still draw a crowd in rural areas — especially if you have small blond children. These people from the local neighborhood are looking through the fence of our school as we celebrate Earth Day on the basketball court. Wow! Look at all those crazy foreigners of all different colors jumping around and having fun. Better than TV.

DAY 59 Red String (Not the Bureaucratic Kind)

The use of "red tape" to bind legal documents goes all the way back to the 16th-century Spanish court of Charles V, and the term became synonymous with unnecessary bureaucracy in 1800s England and America. This plastic red string or rope, however, is used by everyone in China where all and everything is tied together with it. It is cheap (about 50 cents a roll), can be bought anywhere and has a certain springiness that lends itself to binding things together. It is produced in several different colors but the Chinese prefer it red. If you want it green you'll have to go to Thailand. In Chinese folklore there is a "red string of fate" that invisibly binds two people together whose paths are destined to cross in a positive or romantic way.

DAY 58 People's Liberation Army Shoes

Known as *jiefang xie*, "liberation shoes," in Chinese, these sneakers created a nation. Can you imagine the entire armed forces in a country the size of China wearing shoes like this? The army wears green ones and the navy white. Standard issue for the enlisted man and civilian alike. Virtually every peasant, miner and worker wears them, and 30 years ago everyone else did as well. They are cheap (about US$1.50), very durable, have great surface grip, accommodate any width of foot and are sold everywhere. They give poor support, however, and you end up flat-footed after wearing them for many years. Jiefang xie are a definite class divider, now worn only by people who can't afford anything else. Fancy city folk won't touch them. Trendy young foreigners, however, adore them, along with Mao hats sporting red stars (few civilian Chinese would be caught dead wearing that today) and army issue shoulder bags with "Serve The People" stenciled on them. The two latter items are only produced for the foreign tourist market. Recently this homely, modest canvas shoe with the rubber toe protector was exported to the West and is now sold for US$50-75 by a company named Ospop, which has pimped the design just a little to make the shoes even cooler. They are still made in China but are definitely more chic than the ones I can buy in my corner shop. In my opinion, jiefang xie stand for many of the things I love about China and the Chinese laborer — reliable, hardworking, practical, humorous, funky and corny all wrapped into one cool package. I hope they both never go out of style.

DAY 57 Part 1 Money and Superstition

Walked out my gate yesterday evening and this was parked on the sidewalk outside: a Rolls Royce with license plate number 1111. I continued and soon passed a Maserati, a Bentley, a couple of Porsches and a Lamborghini — not an uncommon sight on any day of the week. BMWs are peanuts here, everyone's got one. China is literally ROLLING in big bucks. The enormous conspicuous wealth concentrated in the hands of an elite upper class is mind-blowing. Young beautiful women driving luxurious sports cars as they speak on the latest iPhone are a common sight. They are either daughters or mistresses of rich businessmen. The men or wives have chauffeurs. Many Chinese have also reverted to old superstitious ways that were so looked down upon by the Communist government, one of them a belief in lucky numbers. It is no coincidence that a person who can afford a Rolls has a special number plate that says he is Number 1 four times over. Repetition of any number compounds and accentuates the meaning. The Chinese language is full of homophonic double meanings that numerology relies on. Thus "one," pronounced *yao*, can also mean "want" or "desire." I would say this guy has already "got" what he "wants."

DAY 57 Part 2 The Super Rich

I just had to post a double today along the theme of "those who have much more than they need." This image was taken by my husband on a cross street to the Rolls picture. This 24-year-old young man clearly loves China AND his Ferrari. I love how his shoes match the license plate and his pants the stars of the Chinese flag. On his T-shirt is a picture of Al Pacino in the Godfather. His license plate BB 458 can be interpreted in Sichuan dialect as *bao bei shi wo fa* = "Baby, I'm definitely gonna make it big." Vanity plates like this with special letter-number combinations that can be interpreted in various auspicious ways are common among the rich and are usually purchased at auctions or directly off a list from the government.

DAY 56 Fifty Shades of Grey

We rarely have clear-blue-sky days in Chengdu, so many people tend to forget that we are surrounded by high mountains. The reason why? We live at the bottom of a deep bowl. Just outside the city to the west is the beginning of the Qinghai-Tibetan Plateau, a magnificent geological formation that rises abruptly from the Sichuan Basin and quickly soars to over 5000 meters in elevation. After a storm, in very clear weather and from a tall height, you can see all the way to the peak of Gongga Shan, which is 7,556 meters (24,790 ft) tall. This happens about once every 10 years. On this map we are located on that big train line that is heading north to Xi'an, snug up against the western side of the bowl. The big blue river that enters the basin from the south and continues eastward through a tight mountain range is the mighty Yangtze River and those are the famous Yangtze River Gorges. The Yangtze continues out of the picture across China, where it enters the sea just north of Shanghai. Pretty cool stuff. All those mountains to the west continue to be pushed upward by the Indian sub-continent, which means we get frequent heebie-jeebie earthquakes, big and small. Not so cool — Chengdu gets 250-300 foggy or rainy days a year, and is the place with the least sunshine days in ALL of China. Most of the year it is cloudy and overcast, the sky either white or in winter a dull grey of the absolute least sexy kind. The well-worn adage "Sichuan dogs bark at their own shadows when the sun comes out" is comical, but even I get startled on the rare days when I see mine. All this greyness is like a big wet woolen blanket of depressing sedation. Facts: The population of Chengdu and its administrative areas is just under 15 million people. The entire province has over 80 million. And most of us are all cozily stuck inside this geographic bowl.

泽库　夏河　合作　　　　碌曲　西　　安　　清水　　陇县　麟游　淳　　铜川　　　　三门峡　洛宁
河南蒙古族自治县　临潭　漳县　武山　甘谷　天水　　宝鸡　岐山　咸阳　　西安　洛南　　卢氏　河
　　　　卓尼　岷县　礼县　　　凤县　　　　　　　　　渭南　　　　　商洛　　伏
　　　　迭部　腊子　宕昌　西和　徽县　　　略阳　秦　　洋县　宁陕　石泉　安康　　郧西　丹凤　商南　栾川　牛
久治　阿坝　　　武都　康县　阳平关　汉中　西乡　　　　　安康　　　郧县　丹江口　西峡　山
　　　　九寨沟　　　文县　青川　广元　大　南江　镇巴　岚皋　平利　竹溪　房县　　保康　　神农架林区
红原　松潘　雪宝顶　平武　剑阁　苍溪　巴中　通江　　坪口　竹山　　　兴山湖
毛儿盖　　　　江油　梓潼　　閬中　平昌　宣汉　　　巫溪　　　　三峡大坝
黑水　北州羌族自治县　茂县　绵阳　盐亭　南部　仪陇　达州　开县　云阳　奉节　巫山　西陵峡　宜昌
坝塘　巴尔康　　理县　德阳　三台　西充　　　　　万州　　　巴东　长阳土家族自治县
　大　金川　　都江堰　金堂　南充　广安　　忠县　利川　建始　五峰土家族自治县
沪霍　道孚　小金　　成都　资阳　遂宁　地　华蓥　　石柱土家族　恩施　鹤峰　石门
　四川　　眉山　仁寿　资中　大足　长寿　重庆　宣恩　咸丰　来凤　桑植　张家界　常德
康定　　雅安　洪雅　井研　永川　涪陵　　　　　　　龙山　桃源
峨眉山　乐山　荣县　内江　　　南川　武隆苗族土家族自治县　永顺　　安化
九龙　　峨边彝族自治县　自贡　泸州　　天　道真仡佬族　沅陵　　新化
　　　甘洛　沐川　屏山　宜宾　合江　赤　南　正安苗族自治县　秀山土家族苗族自治县　吉首　冷水江
越西　美姑　雷波　兴　永善　习水　古蔺　茅台　凤冈德江　凤凰　　怀化湖
昭觉　金阳　　威信　　金沙　遵义　湄潭　石阡　思南　苗族侗族自治州　邵
盐源　宁南　昭通　大方　赫章　开阳　余庆　镇远　凯里　侗族自治县　武冈
会东　会泽　威宁彝族回族苗族自治县　纳雍　贵阳　三穗　黎平
华坪　东川　宣威　　　苗族布依族自治　南明　龙公山　从江
永仁　禄劝彝族苗族自治县　寻甸回族　安顺　苗族　独山　龙胜各族自治县
大姚　武定　曲靖　兴仁　贞安　罗甸　　荔波　兴
姚安　　昆明　　龙安　册亨　望谟　从江　福

DAY 55 Tattooed Eyebrows

When I first saw women with tattooed eyebrows in the late 1980s, I was amazed; the concept had never crossed my mind. I thought it was a bold, irreversible thing to do so shortly after a period in China's history when any kind of "fashion" and body beautification was severely punished. Fashion-conscious Chinese women strive for thin but defined brows and as white a skin as possible. Skin whiteners and bleaching lotions are the norm, and this is another class differentiator between country people (who have rough hands and dark skin from working out in the sun) and "citizens" — city dwellers (pale skin and soft hands with long nails from avoiding manual labor). Young and old women do it. You don't need to get the full filled-in tattoo, but can opt for a more natural look that uses semi-permanent ink and a pattern of individual hairs instead of a filled-in shape like these ladies have. The eyebrow tattoos are indeed beautifully arched, but if your natural brow doesn't follow the generic tattooed brow then you need to be assiduous about keeping your brow shaved. Body tattoos in China are otherwise relatively uncommon (but the trend is growing) and usually frowned upon because tattoos are traditionally associated with the criminal world and minority groups.

DAY 54 There Is Something in Your Ear!

Never put anything in your ear smaller than your elbow! Obviously no one has listened to their mother here in Chengdu, where roving ear cleaners stalk customers in public parks and teahouses. While you sit in a bamboo chair enjoying your wonderful leisurely Chengdu life, the ear cleaner announces his approach by twanging his long tuning fork tweezers. His tool kit is quite terrifying when you know that he's aiming to stick 'em in your ear: homemade Q-tips that look like tiny chimney sweeps Bert would have used in Mary Poppins; miniature ear-goo trowels, small scary knives and a nifty spelunking headlamp. Ear cleaning is a Sichuan specialty and for those who dare to have this service performed, it appears to be worth it — all customers I have seen seem to be in a minor state of ecstasy, lying back with a faint smile on their face. The ear cleaner knows his business, as he not only cleans out any gunk you might have but is also trained to manipulate and subtly massage acupuncture points inside the aural cavity. I admit I have not dared to try this myself and feel quite the wimp for it.

DAY 53 Who Gets to Pay the Bill

This is not a perfect picture because I was too consumed with the hilarity of what was happening to time the photo properly. Scenario: Good friend comes to visit. Husband, wife, brother and friend all go out to lunch. Everyone is having a fabulous time, meal is eaten, drinks have been drunk. Time to pay the bill. Friend that was invited out to lunch makes a move toward the cash register to pay the bill and All Hell Breaks Loose. Husband and wife lunge at him and the circus begins. Wife is particularly vehement and vicious, pulling at the friend and berating him verbally. The husband also gets it, as he isn't aggressive enough in getting between friend and cash register. Woman literally goes behind the counter and forbids the cashier to take friend's money. All the while the friend is laughing and the cashier is exasperated. The husband gives up and the woman chases the friend around the restaurant giving him some brutal shoves from behind. She of course wins in the end and all participants in this soap opera settle back happily at the table. Face has been saved — everyone played his or her part to perfection. Another day at a restaurant in China.

DAY 52 Outdoor Newspapers

People's Daily (*Renmin Ribao*) is the official party organ (I love the expression "party organ") of the Communist Party of China and is one of the most influential and important newspapers in the world, with a circulation of several hundred million copies daily. If you want to know the government's official policy on something, this is where you can read it. Every day around the country, it is posted along with other local newspapers behind glass on public display boards like this one in the People's Park in central Chengdu. Not so long ago, these boards were everywhere: in parks, along main roads, by the post office and on the grounds of universities and schools. Such displays make sure that people get the party message, and they are a way to read the news for free. China has some 2200 different daily newspapers. Most young people, however, get their news from the Internet and TV and sift through what they hear, read and are told, and correlate it with the latest postings on any one of China's many popular micro-blogging websites or *weibos.* Internet access is heavily censored, and many sites like Facebook, Wordpress and YouTube are blocked. I like the way these men are standing. When I was a child my mother told me to put my hands behind my back so I wouldn't be tempted to touch anything in a store and risk breaking it. To this day this is how I stand in a store.

DAY 51 Carving Out Space for Yourself

In a country with over 1.4 billion people, how do you find a place to be alone? In China, 95 percent of the people live in 45 percent of its landmass in Eastern and Southern China. Of this population, 52 percent lives in cities and urban areas. There are people everywhere all the time. I am not discussing here the Western vs Asian concept of Personal Space. I am talking about everyone's need to be alone, at least some of the time. Here again there are differences in need according to cultural background and personality. Since actual square footage is at a premium, the Chinese are good at finding space and peace inside their heads. This kind of turning inward and disregarding the world and chaos around you even though it is right in your face is something that I admire and envy. Some people channel it into intellectual pursuits like meditation, taichi, qigong, calligraphy or painting, which all demand a high level of concentration to be successful. Others are copious readers. I find that most Chinese don't actually want to be alone. But for those who do, a common way is to find a slightly secluded corner of a public park and then, just like in the West, "zone out" with a mobile phone. These girls are together but apart, only a few feet away from thousands of other visitors, surrounded by an deafening cacophony of Sunday Park Noise. They have just visited a shop and gotten two "freebie" bags; they are sitting on a company brochure to protect their clothes.

DAY 50 Modern Matchmaking

How do you find a life partner in China? Just because there are a lot of people doesn't mean it is easy. The competition is fierce and young city people today just don't have time to date. Expectations are high on both sides: career, income, social status, level of education are all major factors in deciding who to choose as a spouse. Since the One-Child Policy started in 1979, there has been a surplus of eligible men in their 20s and 30s, so finding a "suitable" wife is difficult. Chinese women today are better educated and many are quite satisfied with their single life and have no interest in rushing into a marriage, where they risk falling back into old roles of cooking, cleaning, child-rearing and looking after aging parents. One solution — in the minds of the parents — is the establishment of open-air marriage markets like this one in Chengdu's People's Park. Parents (rarely the children themselves) describe their offspring's various attributes (height, what zodiac animal they are born under, income, apartment or no apartment, education level, driver's license, etc.) and hang the written description on trees or sticks stuck in the ground. Many mothers and fathers come to scrutinize the information and call and arrange dates between their child and a presumptive spouse. Professional matchmakers work the crowds as well, seeking a commission. It seems that the success rate is low, yet these parents are unwilling to give up anytime soon, with such high hopes of securing happiness and a future family for their child.

DAY 49 Foot Massage

Chinese culture takes a holistic approach to health and well-being. One of the more pleasurable ways of partaking in thousands of years of acquired knowledge is getting a foot massage. Foot reflexology massage relies on meridian and pressure points in the foot because these points are thought to be connected to all organs in the body. A foot massage is not for the ticklish or sensitive. You will come away from a two-hour session not feeling all cozy, like after a Thai massage, but feeling like you have been served a great whack of very hard love. First your feet are soaked in scalding hot herbal-infused water as your head and upper body are pummeled aggressively. Then oil or cream is applied as pressure points are thoroughly examined and massaged with muscular gusto to determine if you have any problems in the rest of your body. Great expertise is at work here and any physical problems you might have are loudly discussed and dissected with the other masseurs/masseuses in the room. After the feet come the legs and thighs, and if you are lucky a wonderful gluteus maximus massage. When finished your circulation is going gangbusters, your *qi* is restored, your hair looks like hell and you have had a hilarious time discussing your health with your masseur, who has served you the straight dope on everything from the state of your spleen to how horrible your heels look — that's when the man with the spelunking lamp and sharp scalpel comes in and carefully shaves away your callouses. A Chinese foot massage is not for the squeamish.

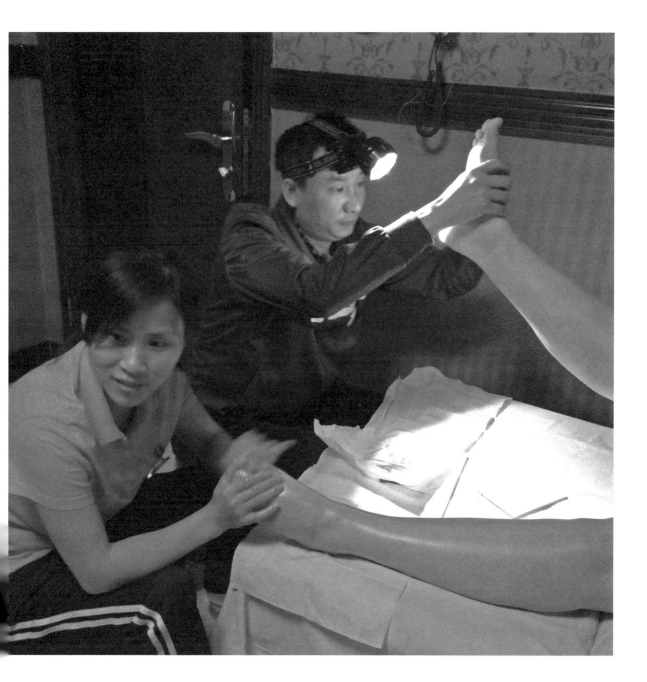

DAY 48 Get Down and Boogie

Can you have more fun than people do in China's public parks? Anything to get out of the apartment, get some air and see some greenery. Every weekend from sunup to sundown you can dance, do aerobics, learn how to waltz and tango, sing your heart out, find a partner at the Marriage Market, air out your songbird and let him meet his friends, find a quiet corner and catch up on your knitting, take the grandkid for a stroll, drink a cup of tea, get your ears cleaned, perfect your water calligraphy, catch up with friends, hijack a foreigner and practice your English, sneak off to a secluded corner and canoodle with your lover, go crazy in a rowboat, or examine the orchids, peonies, chrysanthemums or whatever else is in bloom. China's public parks are heaving with humanity on the weekends and deliver some of the best people watching you will find anywhere in the world.

DAY 47 More Hijinks at the People's Park

Boating for 30 minutes with friends and family is both hilariously fun and very stressful, as rowing skills are not a priority in today's China; nor can everyone swim. And too many people are sharing too small a space. I have had numerous heated discussions with my children at this park about who was the captain and who was an idiot and didn't know a thing about rowing. After almost bludgeoning each other with our hefty oars, we usually made it across the pond, under the bridge, and around the island and back without crashing into too many people, and at the same time providing the locals with huge entertainment as we shouted heatedly at each other and honed our repertoire of expletives in several languages. All the while my husband sat in the back of the boat and never said a peep. Clever him.

DAY 46 Hot Boiled Water

One is never far from a source of boiled water in China. Hot drinking water keeps the country going, just as coffee is the foundation that Sweden stands on. Everyone carries a water bottle or thermos flask, containing boiled water or tea. The tall Nescafe glass jar with the sturdy brown lid used to be the fashion statement in China, as it cost a lot to buy the coffee in the first place. It also signaled that you knew someone who liked a foreign drink. Grannies crocheted smart little mesh stockings to carry this jar in so it wasn't dropped and broken. Still a popular choice among taxi drivers, they are kept between the two front seats. Thermoses like these are owned by almost every Chinese and are a must for the dorm student. A matching pair is a common wedding gift in the countryside. Longtime China watchers yearn nostalgically for the flasks of 20 years ago: cheap metal ones with a simple cork, stenciled with big lush pink peonies or bright swimming carp. The vacuum flask inside was fragile and would often break as you made your way to the boiler room of the student dormitory or hotel you were staying in. Once filled, the corks often popped out because the water was so hot. Nowadays most city people don't worry about boiling water. Instead they have bottled water delivered to their homes, which can be boiled or chilled in a dispenser. Drinking icy cold water is a relatively new phenomenon because cold liquids are deemed dangerous to health. One often hears quasi-scientific explanations such as "cold water solidifies fats in your stomach, thus clogging up your digestion" or "cold water doesn't mix well with hot food." Young people have thrown many of these old notions to the wind and happily slurp on an icy cold green tea Frappuccino at Starbucks.

DAY 45 Wave to the People!

In the center of Chengdu there once stood a lovely palace built in the Ming Dynasty "official building" cookie-cutter architectural style, of which the Forbidden City in Beijing is the loveliest and most magnificent example: multiple courtyards with ever-more-lavish multi-eaved buildings raised up on platforms, one after the other, surrounded by protective walls and a moat. In 1967-1968 this complex that stood upon the original site of a palace from the Shu Kingdom (almost 2000 years ago) was dynamited and destroyed in the political fervor of the Cultural Revolution. The moat around it was filled in to make an air-raid shelter. Zealots erected a Mao statue approximately at the spot where the old palace entrance gate stood, in an attempt to emulate the political enthusiasm of those who erected the first Mao statue at Beijing's Qinghua University in 1967. A memorial hall was built behind him that later, in the 1980s, became an exhibition hall for Sichuan's best products. This later became the Science and Technology Museum of today. Before 2006, when Tianfu Square was constructed at his feet, this huge statue of Mao towered over the top end of People's Road South, with a height of 30 meters (100 feet) and a huge outstretched hand. Indeed, this particular Mao statue stands as one of the most famous of the 2000 such statues that were erected all over the country during the height of the Cultural Revolution (1966-1976). Chengdu has two, this one and one on the grounds of Sichuan University. This Mao is hardly noticed today because he is dwarfed by the enormous "Ode to the Glory of Sichuan" sculpture that dominates Tianfu Square. A highly controversial figure historically, but many people — particularly the elderly — still respect him. Here, however, the man who so moved China hardly makes a wave.

DAY 44 Land of Ents

It is a common sight in China to see a tree passing by. But unlike an Ent, it is not walking but driving past on the back of a truck. Most trees are transported upright, so it does feel like they are alive and out for a stroll. Housing and commercial development is expanding so rapidly in China that few people have time to let a tree grow and mature naturally. They are brought in fully grown, plunked into a hole and propped up on all sides with the hope that they will take root and not die. Landscape architects rarely take into account natural growth, planning their developments around an old tree or waterway. Trees that are "in the way," like this one, are dug out of the ground and sold off to be moved elsewhere. A mature tree fetches quite a lot of money. Entire villages are razed to make way for new "development" and the new is always symmetrical and carefully mapped out. The feeling of something that has organically grown and developed out of the past with all its eccentricities, personality quirks and historical attachments is virtually nonexistent in today's China, with its straight roads and shiny new worlds. Each city looks just like the next, and so do the transplanted trees.

DAY 43 Street Cleaners

China's workplace death rate far exceeds that of most developed countries; for example, it is 21 times more common to have a fatal accident at work in China than in the UK. One thinks of construction workers and miners, but street cleaners and roadway workers are particularly prone to fatal injuries by being hit by cars. On my way to work every day I think about these men and women as they calmly go about their business sweeping the streets and polishing the dividers and barriers on freeways and highways, often with only inches between them and motorists. They wear orange vests or jackets and appear quite visible, but are still in danger because of the chaotic traffic situation in China, where drivers disregard traffic signs, rules and regulations and rush in any direction deemed the shortest or best route. Vehicles blithely back up on freeways, head the wrong way down one-way streets, swerve out into traffic without looking, run red lights, expect all other traffic to give way and ignore bicycles and motor scooters entirely. It is the poorest of the poor who become street cleaners, usually former farmers and country folk who might even have lived and farmed on the very land that now supports the new super highway with its terrible drivers.

DAY 42 The People Who Make It Happen

These builders are the people who are making Modern China. The ones who work all through the night on construction sites in every corner of the country. The ones who sleep in temporary dormitory housing, showering in communal showers and eating canteen food. The ones who spend the entire year away from their children and families, sending money home to the grandparents so the children can go to school, get an education and not have to toil as a construction workers. The ones who travel across the country at Chinese New Year to visit their families just once a year. The ones who earn only a few hundred US dollars per month and who save most of it. Most of them wear Liberation sneakers (Day 58), yellow hardhats and regular clothing as their only safety gear. They carry their tools back and forth during meal breaks and off-hours and are at constant risk of a workplace accident. Women work at heavy labor as much as the men. These people might not be the investors or visionaries who are creating New China, but they are the ones physically making it happen. And every year more and more of them are becoming just a little bit better off, able to leave their life of burden and move permanently away from the construction site to a city apartment.

DAY 41 Chinese Men Carry Their Girlfriends' Handbags

This picture isn't unusual or uncommon. You see it every day and everywhere no matter what age the man is or whether he is holding the girlfriend's or the wife's bag. Even Chinese leader Xi Jinping was photographed carrying First Lady Peng Liyuan's purse on a recent foreign trip. He was touted as "the best husband in China" and "the model of a Chinese man" until the image was revealed to be photoshopped. Why do men do this? Are Chinese males controlled by their women? Are they less masculine than Western men? Or is it the other way around, they want to control everything their ladies do and never venture from their side? A number of Chinese friends, male and female, told me that it is done out of kindness and love. One friend even went so far as to say that since gender roles are still imbalanced in China, this is one way for Chinese men to show deference to women. It is a kind of compensation. The men feel in no way sexually diminished or controlled, and since everyone does it no one thinks twice about it. Chinese women don't feel their men are less "men" for toting their bags, but equally not all Chinese women ask their men to do this. There is a saying in the local Sichuan dialect: *pa er duo* — "soft ear." It is said about a man who is slightly subservient to his wife, deferring to her and taking care of her. In China the most "controlled men" (i.e., in many Chinese women's eyes, the best husbands) are perceived to be men from Sichuan and Shanghai. They cook, clean and take care of the children more than others. Stereotypes for sure, but where there's smoke there's fire.

DAY 40 Lucky Haircuts

The *Er Yue Er* Festival (Second Day of the Second Lunar Month) is one of the busiest days of the year for Chinese barbers because this is the day when the Dragon Raises Its Head (*Longtaitou*), meaning that it is an auspicious day to get a haircut. Get a good haircut and you will be lucky for the rest of the year. This little boy has a lucky star at the back of his head and the Apple company logo on his crown (unseen). A few months have passed since his head was shaved and he seemed oblivious to the wishful thinking of his parents, scooting along on a push-car in a working-class section of Chengdu. Apples symbolize wisdom in China and of course your one and only child is absolutely a superstar.

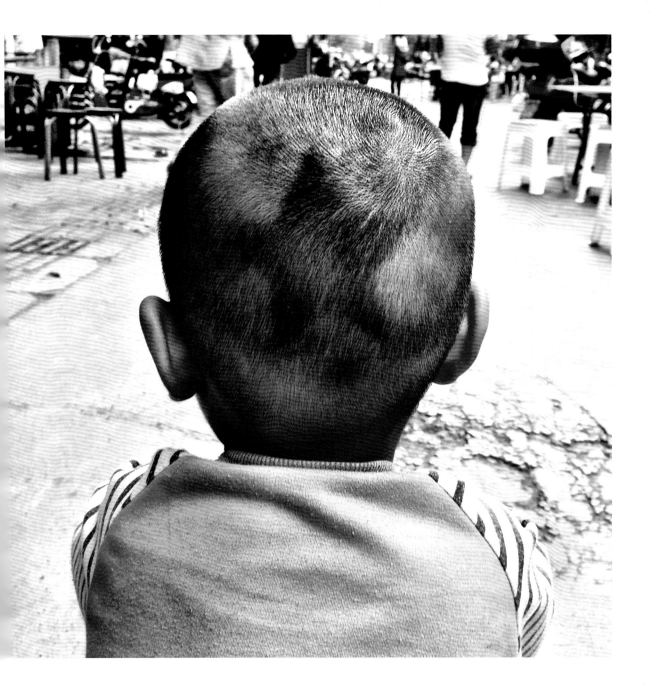

DAY 39 Split Pants

Most Chinese babies wear *kai dang ku* (open-crotch pants) from birth, with a towel tucked in that is changed frequently. Since the mid-1990s, Western style disposable diapers have been available in places like Beijing, Shanghai and Guangzhou. Now they are available all over the country, with the greatest increase of users in the cities and among the better-off families — diapers are expensive. Many Chinese parents, however, still prefer the much cheaper split pants and also consider them to be both healthier for their children and absolutely better for the environment. With split pants you pay nothing extra and the babies and toddlers seldom have rashes or infections, even in wintertime when they instead wear several layers of them. When the time comes, children are potty-trained by the "elimination communication" method, whereby the parent, or usually grandparent, holds the baby between his or her legs, spreads the baby's legs and makes a "shhhh" sound that encourages the baby to urinate. The baby gets used to this sound and easily connects it to "now it's time to pee." Chinese children are usually "dry" by 2 years of age or younger. The downside is that it demands a lot of time on the part of the parents, who frequently have to make sure the baby has just peed and won't "make a mistake." The really horrible side in the eyes of foreigners is not all the cute bare bottoms you see in China, but how Chinese parents and grandparents allow their toddlers to squat and pee and poop everywhere and anywhere. And I mean that literally: inside train compartments, on restaurant floors, in stores, in airport lounges and anywhere out on the streets. Indeed, Chinese children get used to doing their business in public, and you can see older children squatting by the roadside in full view of all and sundry.

DAY 38 What's That on Your T-shirt?

"Late night angel weenie," "Junky juicy hotdog" — the list is endless. Walk down almost any street in China and you will find yourself chuckling. Since the 1980s, when people started wearing more attention-grabbing (i.e., non-utilitarian) apparel, fashion has developed rapidly in China. From being the root of all things evil and corrupting, Western tastes and ideas suddenly became extremely attractive. There were a few blips along the way — the anti-Spiritual Pollution Campaign of 1983 and the anti-Bourgeois Liberalization Campaign of the late 1980s — where wearing jeans and listening to Taiwanese pop music could actually land you in jail or a labor camp. Horrible. After such political movements died down, clothing and bags with text began invading China through Hong Kong, with foreign backpackers and young overseas Chinese visiting the Mainland. Local manufacturers quickly caught on, but their English didn't. Now any text written in the Roman alphabet and in English seems just about the coolest thing possible. Even if the seat of your pants says "Fuck me" or your T-shirt says "Prostitute," it looks cool. Most people are unaware of what the words actually mean. A parallel in the West is the proliferation of Chinese character tattoos, where only your trust in the tattoo artist or your proficiency in Chinese guarantees that you too don't wear something that says you look like a fool.

DAY 37 Going, Going, GONE

If you see this large red character written on a building you won't be seeing that building for much longer, because *chai* means "demolish." This character, usually circled and seen sloppily painted on buildings all over China, has caused huge amounts of anxiety and controversy over the years because the owners or renters of the buildings, or homes themselves, have little to say about the coming demolition. Recently the government has tried to move away from using the character chai (as in *chaiqian*, "demolition and removal") and toward the more benign characters for "relocation" (*banqian*). The chai word here is on a large building near our apartment complex. The ground floor is populated by small shops and private businesses selling DIY home decoration products: paint, wood, fixtures, toilets etc. They have serviced the many apartments that were built in the Europe City complex next door and the thousands of private apartments in the adjacent Tongzilin area. Indeed, it is convenient to have them so close when you need a light bulb, a lock fixed, a new faucet, toilet or bucket of wall paint. The building is shabby and run-down, though the land under it is quite precious. It is only a matter of time until the wrecking crew arrives and a new apartment high-rise will appear in its place. The small shop owners will relocate, probably further out on the outskirts of town, and life will go on. We will have to shop at the impersonal but large and efficient chain store B&Q.

DAY 36 China Has a Big Appetite

In a country of over 1.4 billion people with a rapidly expanding middle class, a lot of cash changes hands and people can't seem to spend it fast enough. Shopping malls, department stores, car dealerships, furniture stores, fancy shoe shops, apartment complexes, start-up companies, travel agents, theme parks, restaurants. The amount of goods and services that are generated and consumed every year has never before been witnessed in the history of mankind. Some of the biggest consumers are teenagers and young adults. They have no siblings, they still live at home and they have six adults doting on them. Any income is spent on themselves, as many of them pay for nothing at home. It is common for a 20-something-year-old to spend his/her entire monthly wage on one designer bag or a new smartphone. There has also been a shift from "things" to "experiences." The travel industry is exploding, as can be seen by the dramatic increase in Chinese tourists around the world. The Chinese consumer equates a high price with better quality. If something is cheap, then it must also be of poorer quality. The thinking is "you get what you pay for." By over-simplifying, one can say there are two kinds of city people in China: those who will pay exorbitant amounts of money for flashy designer goods and big brand names (the ones who buy the Maseratis and Lamborghinis and US$2,000 purses), and those who will do everything to look like they have bought these goods but can only afford the fake ones. This car packed to the gills with ladies' purses was parked outside the local Hongqi (Red Flag) convenience store. A brisk business was going on and the car owner had one eye on the customers and one eye on any approaching police. How he could even drive the car to this location is beyond me.

DAY 35 Superstition

China is a tough place to be. You need all the help you can get. Competition is sharp, so to maintain your edge over everyone else you have to work hard, keep your eyeballs peeled for the next deal or advantage, have good contacts and keep the gods happy. The god here is the three-legged Money Toad - *Jin Cha* or *Chan Cha*. Like the popular Beckoning Cat (the Japanese Maneki Neko), he's all about money, a thing foremost on people's minds. This big ugly sucker has a gold coin in his mouth, three legs (not four), a string of "cash" coins and the Seven Stars of the Big Dipper in bright-colored astral pearls on his back. His purpose is to guard the entrance to your store, restaurant or home and make sure money comes in but not out. He is a harbinger of good luck and is a powerful fengshui master. Jin Cha comes in all sizes and keeps company with the Heavenly Immortals — he's a good friend to have.

DAY 34 Part 1 Giant Pandas

The taxis in Chengdu have a recorded voice that greets you upon entering the vehicle: "Welcome to Chengdu, Home of Pandas and Land of Bandits." Did I hear that correctly? Bandits? Perhaps … but none of us has been able to figure out what the lady is actually saying. Panda City — absolutely. In Chengdu we do pandas like no one else. Every taxi has a panda painted on its side, we sell Panda Brand cigarettes, there is a Panda Prince Hotel, and a giant panda dancing on a pillar welcomes us at Shuangliu International Airport. At one time Chengdu actually wanted to officially change its 2000-year-old name to Panda City. Thankfully that didn't happen, but we are still the capital of Pandaville. The Chengdu Research Base of Giant Panda Breeding is located on the edge of the city. It is a great place, a wonderful green oasis, where researchers have successfully gotten pandas to reproduce — albeit with lots of scientific help and prodding in the nether regions. The entrance ticket gives these pointers: "Please stay quiet, do not tease, chase after or beat up animals. Do not smoke in the base. Do not feed the animals for their safety. Do not bring your pets within. Do not step into giant panda's enclosure for they are very offensive." Well, no pandas were offensive today when I paid a visit to the panda reserve. Lethargic from the heat, they were hanging limply in trees like big sodden woolen blankets. The staff had to drag them down from the trees and carry them into air-conditioned rooms.

DAY 34 Part 2 Red Pandas

The attractive little red pandas are quite different from their distant cousins the giant panda, and more closely resemble a North American raccoon. Very active, they like to roam on the forest floor or nimbly climb up into the lofty trees to stretch out and look down at what's happening below, or to espy what they can possibly eat or avoid. On the ground they walk pigeon-toed and flat-footed and have a lumbering, albeit speedy gait that closely resembles the motions of a bear. Here at the Panda Base outside of Chengdu they are bred in great numbers and have free range of their multiple stockades, nimbly passing from enclosure to enclosure through little holes in the chain-link fence. They are completely used to the loud tourists who come to see them every day, walking between or beside them in an attempt to get on with their day. The Eastern Himalayas and Southwest China are home to the red panda; our nearby Wawu Mountain is said to be a particularly good place to see one in the wild. There are only about 10,000 of these magnificent animals left in the world today, so treat them kindly!

DAY 33 One-Child Policy

This girl most likely doesn't have a brother or sister. She's riding on the freeway with her mother, holding a computer hard drive in her lap. No helmet. Not on her way to school, as she isn't wearing the ubiquitous school uniform of blue and white gym suit and red Young Pioneer scarf. They've got a red raincoat and a bottle of green tea drink in the front basket. Mom has her jacket draped over the steering wheel, ready to wear back to front to protect her nice clothes from traffic grime. The girl is holding on to Mom but she actually has a small back support in the jump seat of this scooter, commonly used to transport the "one" child back and forth to school. China's One-Child Policy began in 1979 and has been successful to the point of being a problem. China is now a nation of sibling-less people, no cousins or aunts and uncles. That means lots of adults concentrating all of their hopes, love and desires on one person. Many children become spoiled, cossetted and even obese. The divorce rate among young married couples is high, as this is perhaps the first time they have had to think of someone else's feelings and needs. It is an interesting polemic. China has a gargantuan task organizing a population of over 1.4 billion people. With limited resources and a fast-growing economy, it's amazing how well things work. It is a country with enormous forward momentum. The policy doesn't strictly adhere to one child for all. There are many exceptions: non-Han are allowed to have one or more children. Rural families whose first child is a girl, or handicapped, may have another. If you divorce and remarry someone who is childless you may also have another. Since 2013 the policy has been relaxed so that families are allowed two children if both parents are single children. At present most people still stick to one child due to the high costs of raising children in China.

DAY 32 Beggars

It's not easy being old or poor, or disabled, sick or deformed. Many whose life this is wind up begging on the streets. When meeting a beggar you must make a decision. Give money? Give food? Look the other way and walk on? Beggars in China are generally scorned, yet many people readily give them small amounts of money. This might be because of a religious belief, a conscious moral decision, a feeling of fear, pressure, general humanity or relief that "if not for the grace of Guanyin, that could be me." Beggars are found all over China, and come in all shapes and sizes and have all kinds of motivations. Some are indeed "professionals" who make their money solely from begging when they are absolutely capable of holding a regular job. They can be scarily aggressive, targeting the weak and particularly foreigners. There are also awful stories of organized criminal gangs that kidnap countryside children or hoodwink destitute parents into believing their children will be taken care of, and then physically and mentally abuse them and force them into begging. Many beggars, however, have little choice in a developing country like China. It is an old tradition for the blind to work as itinerant musicians, playing the *erhu* or *pipa* and walking the streets with a relative or helper, begging along the way. No matter "real" beggar or "fake" beggar; as my children say: "It is a horrible thing to have to walk the streets for endless hours, or lie facedown on the payment with a sign asking for a donation; the humiliation of begging should always be considered and most beggars should at least be treated with respect."

DAY 31 Dead Heroes Make the Best Heroes

The man in the red winter hat is Lei Feng. Like James Dean and Che Guevara, he is a convenient DEAD hero. Orphaned early with no parents to lay claim to him, he died at the age of 21 in a ridiculous tragi-comic accident whilst a soldier in the People's Liberation Army. Young dead heroes are perfect for myth building. Virtually anything can be constructed about their so-called deeds. They themselves are not there to trip themselves up. They don't grow old to make mistakes and become corrupt and fat like everyone else. After Lei Feng died his diary was conveniently "found," wherein it was "discovered" that he was a veritable treacle tart of goodie two shoe-ness. Lei Feng embodied the perfect citizen devoted to clean living, Socialism, Mao Zedong and the Chinese people. The Communist party propaganda machine hijacked his death and soon trotted him out as a person to emulate in the "Follow the examples of Comrade Lei Feng Campaign" of 1963. Since then he has waxed and waned as a role model for all to follow, with the result that many people today couldn't care less about Lei Feng and find him quite the joke. In this picture he is promoting "modernism" and "development," i.e., "come buy an apartment in our new housing complex."

DAY 30 Small Is Good

I don't have any statistics on the millions of enterprises that are run by one person and his or her immediate family. Just as important as the millions of small and medium-sized businesses with fewer than 100 employees, these "hole-in-the-wall" trades are very much what makes China tick. This seamstress has set up shop under a stairwell. She has enclosed the space with a door that can be locked, she has a fridge behind her and a bed tucked away directly under the stair incline. Customers can sit outside on the rough chairs, and she can eat her meals at the simple table. She services the migrant workers who are building the South Railway Station a few hundred meters away, repairing their clothes and luggage, sewing bedding, etc. I don't know if she has any children or a husband, but I have seen other seamstresses living under stairs with their families; the child plays in front of the shop and the husband works as a construction worker or day laborer. This woman comes from the countryside beyond the city of Chengdu. This entire street is full of small businesses: hardware shop, dumpling and noodle shop, small convenience store, cobbler, hairdresser, "massage" ladies, etc. When the South Station is finished the street and all its businesses will disappear and everyone will relocate to some other place in China where something new is being built and their many talents are needed. They earn little money yet can survive and even save a little bit.

DAY 29 Too Big Is Not Good

China is obsessed with BIG, and Chengdu — being the fourth-largest city in China — is no slacker in this category. It currently lays claim to the world's largest stand-alone building. The New Century Global Centre is 500 meters long and 400 meters wide, with 1.9 million square meters of floor space. It claims to be big enough to hold 20 Sydney Opera Houses. Does anyone really care? The interior is filled with name brand shops, a hotel, a movie complex, a glass walkway, an indoor waterpark with fake beach, an inordinate number of coffee shops and few customers. It is also incredibly ugly and gaudy, full of contrasting marble patterns, shiny gold metal banisters, crystal chandeliers, lots of glass that will never be cleaned, fake palm trees and other dust-collecting plastic vegetation. China has many stunning modern architectural wonders but this is definitely not one of them. I can't wait until some other city is gripped by hysteria and constructs an even bigger, totally unnecessary edifice to the glory of nouveau riche hubris. This building is beneath Chengdu's dignity.

DAY 28 The Mao Suit

Talk about a blast from the past! This man is a walking fashion ode to a bygone era. He is wearing a Zhongshan tunic (known in the West as a Mao suit), a Mao cap (Liberation cap in Chinese), black cloth shoes and white socks and he carries a black satchel over his shoulder. He even sports a wispy Daoist/Ho Chi Minh beard (*shanyang hu* in Chinese = "goat's beard"). Almost no one dresses like this in China today. In the countryside, for sure, many men still sport a green or blue Mao suit because they are sturdy and last almost forever. They've also got four practical pockets and good buttons. A Mao suit in the city screams "Bumpkin! Poor!" A Mao cap is still popular but never with a red star. The suit was popularized in the 1910s by Sun Zhongshan (Sun Yat-sen), the first president of China, who had seen a nifty jacket worn by military cadets in Japan. He combined this style with a Western suit and invented something uniquely "Modern China." Chairman Mao wore his all the time and it is his image and newspaper photos of the toiling masses in similar (cheaper) suits that imprinted it on our minds as the cookie-cutter couture of the Chinese Communist masses. Modern designers have tweaked the suit even more and celebrities like Jacky Chan and Jet Li will wear super fancy black silk versions, but with a much sexier cut than the proletarian ancestor.

DAY 27 Friends

Many good things in this picture make me think "China." Friends, you can't live without them. Eat alone, why? Never. Red plastic chairs? Could be the blue ones as well, but we love plastic chairs. Eat outside despite what the government says about it being a sign of poverty and low class. No way! We love eating outside when the weather is good. Green bottles of Snow Brand beer? What's Chengdu without it?! Back street life, YES! I love Chengdu.

DAY 26 Flower Vendors

In the post-Cultural Revolution 1980s Chengdu was one of the few places in China that allowed itself the audacious frivolity of cut flowers. Yunnan had its wonderful camellias and bougainvillea-clad houses but Yunnan was considered half barbarian anyway. Southern China couldn't help but have wild tropical flowers. The former Imperial Gardens of Beijing sported a few hardy peonies in the spring, but nothing like the insane color profusion they display today. In Chengdu a private person could actually buy flowers to decorate his home. At that time they were sold from the back of Flying Pigeon and Phoenix brand bicycles. In the sea of faded blue-grey-green Mao suits of the 1980s, these bursts of color cycling by exhilarated casual visitors and residents alike. Today the flowers are still transported in cut-off bamboo stocks filled with water and sold from the back of an electric scooter. They are a sure sign of spring and still only cost a pittance.

DAY 25 Valet Parking

If you're going out to your favorite club, massage parlor or restaurant and you're driving a Porsche, Lamborghini, Ferrari, Maserati, MG, Rolls, Bentley or modest BMW, these guys will gladly park your car for you. In front of any establishment worth its salt you will find a small army of neatly dressed, clean-cut young men who make sure customers can arrive in style and not have to worry about parking space being so dear in China. The valets wait under an umbrella or shade tree with their plank of chits and are masters at squeezing in yet another fancy-pants vehicle between all the others that line the streets. You don't have to tip them, but you can if you want; they are paid a monthly wage. Another service some offer (off the books) is to drive you home if you have drunk too much alcohol and can't drive yourself. Of course some owners have their own drivers who wait for them while they are having fun. But the cars still need to be parked somewhere, and the sidewalk is usually the place of choice. It's illegal of course but restaurant and club owners bribe the local police and metermaids (yes, they do exist in China) to look the other way, thus turning an entire block into a multi-million dollar sardine can. The valets are usually crackerjack drivers but once my husband witnessed a newbie mistakenly reverse a Lamborghini into a wall. Oops.

DAY 24 Love

What more needs to be said? I love my iPhone too.

DAY 23 Bare Bellies

It's official. It's summer. The shirts are rolled up and the winter-grey stomachs are bared. Chinese men walk around like this all summer, absentmindedly rubbing their "buddha" bellies without a care in the world. Sometimes the shirt is rolled up all the way over the shoulders. They are called *banye* in Chinese — "exposing grandfathers" — but they are men of all ages and sizes. Sexy it is not.

DAY 22 Riding Sidesaddle

Put on some high-heeled shoes and hike up your dress. Hold on to your man (and your Coke) and zoom away. The road is your playground and the city is your life. Let's go shopping and dream our days away.

DAY 21 Face Masks

Until recently, only those suffering a cold in winter wore a face mask, but now the usage has exploded in China because of the heavy, hazardous air pollution. The past year has seen sales of over 1 billion masks, most in the 1 yuan per mask quality range. Most masks bought in China give little more than psychological support because they do not protect against particles smaller than PM2.5 (particulate matter of 2.5 micrometers). This young woman is purchasing food skewers from a street vendor, whereby she is exposing herself to yet another health risk — recycled food oil called "gutter oil."

DAY 20 Doors

China is a land of doors, walls and barriers, imaginary or actual. High walls traditionally surround courtyard homes. Spirit walls and screens block evil spirits and outside observers from a view into a private realm. Doormen guard entrances to housing estates and compounds. Closed faces reveal no emotions. In China it is often impossible to know what is beyond a facade. But a door can also reveal a little about the inhabitants on the other side. This apartment door is a venue for protective amulets normally changed each year at Chinese New Year. Spring Couplets frame the door left and right with a "four character" distillation of their meaning above the lintel. On the door itself is the single character *fu*, "happiness," inverted as a visual pun: to "turn upside down," *dao*, rhymes with *dao*, "to arrive." Thus anything that passes through the door brings good luck as well as happiness. For the Dragon Boat Festival (*Duanwu Jie*), fresh calamus and mugwort have been hung beside the door. Calamus is Number One of the Five Plants That Protect Against Evil and Disease. The scent of calamus is also good for keeping away bugs and insects. Few young people in China today understand the archaic meanings and connections behind these customs. Usually older couples decorate their door like this.

DAY 19 Traffic Accidents

It is a wonder they don't happen more often because traffic in a large Chinese city is intense, with vehicles, people and vendors everywhere and rampant disregard for traffic rules. Moving objects come from all directions at all times and drivers and pedestrians both need extra vigilance to escape being run over, dragged underneath a passing bus, clipped by a silent electric bike or blatantly run down by a drunk driver. Unsafe sidewalks are often blocked by illegally parked cars, forcing one to walk in the street. Luckily, the urban traffic flows slowly so accidents that look bad are rarely lethal. This motorbike was hit by the car and both are left in place to await either the police or the insurance company. They will not be moved out of the flow of traffic (creating in themselves another traffic hazard) until the matter is resolved. People and cars will just weave around them for the time being. Most minor traffic accidents are resolved on the spot by paying cash. Punishment for drunk driving, however, is severe in China, though the rich and powerful have resuscitated an age-old practice to avoid prison. They hire "body doubles" to stand in for them at trial and even in jail. It is called *ding zui*, substitute crime.

DAY 18 The Jumbly Man Has Arrived!

Feather dusters, rat traps, back scratchers, mops, combs, brooms and dust pans, clothes hangers, scrub brushes, shoe polishers, potato peelers, toilet plungers, fly swatters, bottle cleaners, shoe laces and shoe inserts, you name it, the Jumbly Man has it. In winter he sells Spring Festival decorations: red lanterns, red packets, spring couplets and door decorations; and in the summer he bikes around with household must-haves that save your day in a pinch. Most of the things are handmade in home cottage industries and won't last many seasons, but who cares, it's fun to stand and chew the fat with the Jumbly Man. He's got good gossip, too, and likes to hang out with the fruit sellers. When he's been around in one place too long he hops on his bike and moves to another street corner, calling out his wares along the way. I love his extra-long rooster-tail feather dusters for those hard-to-reach spider webs. And everything costs next to nothing. Oh, Jumbly Man, I'll miss you!

DAY 17 The Delight of Strangers

In 1985, on my 25th birthday, I set out on a 10-day journey across Sweden, Finland and the Soviet Union to China via the Trans-Siberian Railway. I crossed the border at Manzhouli, so technically it was the Trans-Manchurian route. I had dreamt of coming to China ever since I was a small girl in California. I crossed the border in the middle of the night and my first encounter with a "real" Chinese was with a middle-aged man selling souvenir stamps in the Chinese border shop. You can imagine the reaction of a young American, who had first encountered Soviet Russia and now a real live Chinese communist. I was petrified and exhilarated at the same time, and blurted out one of the few things I knew in Chinese, never actually believing that anyone would ever understand what I was saying. "You're Chinese!" I exclaimed. "Of course I'm Chinese," he answered, exasperated but patient. After that he smiled and I smiled, and I actually understood what he said. I think I've been in love with China ever since. So this picture is dedicated to all the chance encounters in which people who really don't understand each other choose to laugh and smile rather than scowl and turn away.

DAY 16 Super Grannies

I don't know if you know it, but this lady is dressed in Sichuan Super Granny haute couture. From the ground up she is about as up-to-date as can be: Soft comfy shoes lined with thick polyester faux fur, more suitable for indoor wear but worn outside by everyone during winter months. Black unisex trousers and blue modified Mao jacket bulging because of the 4-5 layers of woolen underwear and jumpers and sweaters worn underneath. Hand-carved wooden cane. The *piece de la resistance* that totally identifies this woman as a species common to Sichuan Province is the dark red knitted mushroom beret. Classic Chuan Couture. This notion of wearing thick layers of clothing keeps people warm throughout the bitter cold and damp Chinese winter, and lasts far into the year until the traditional calendar states that spring has come (no matter how hot it actually is) and you can downsize your clothing. A bit crazy, but the Chinese have been around a long while and they get a lot of things right no matter what we think. This lady is pushing 90 and is hanging out in front of the local pharmacy. Behind her is a bottle of green tea. She's all set for a great day of checking out the local action.

DAY 15 The Old Dudes Abide

I've got a thing for old Chinese men. I want them all to be my grandfather. Actually my Cuban grandfather was just like them, tootling about town doing his own thing. This guy here is parked outside "Europe City," where lots of rich folks live. He either just delivered something or is waiting to deliver a load somewhere else. China couldn't function without these deliverymen, who work all over the country moving things to and fro for very small sums. He has a homemade wooden box on the front to hold tools and personal items. Sacks and cardboard are in the back to pad things. Pant legs are rolled up of course; it's summertime. His Mao cap is a little niftier than most, more like a Greek fisherman's cap — only we're 2,000 km from the sea.

DAY 14 Shop Names

What can you buy in the GOD shop? Clots? A shop that sounds like "enema"? The "English" names of Chinese stores can be disconcerting, misleading and sometimes just plain hysterical to a foreign eye. These are all nice clothing boutiques in our neighborhood. Made-up French- and Italian-sounding names are also popular for fashion stores. Many times a shop name seems to be taken out of thin air, like "Yoox." What does that mean? It has no connection to its Chinese name, it's just cool to have something foreign-sounding above the door.

DAY 13 Communist Red, White and Blue

A couple of things to note. First, this is a Bank of China local branch that is being renovated. Renovation and remodeling are common and frequent. You can easily go on vacation and come back one month later to see your favorite shop or restaurant replaced by a completely new one, and no one has a clue as to what happened to the shop or its staff. The amount of cement, tile and stone dust, toxic chemicals, and glues that are circulating in the air is frightening — a constant element in Chinese cities. Second, the special cloth that covers the façade is a woven plastic material used as a tarpaulin or an awning, commonly sewn into large bags known as *bian zhi dai*, which Chinese use to stuff their quilts and pillows into, or which function as cheap suitcases preferred by migrant workers. For me the memory of endless lines of Chinese émigrés crossing the border over the Lowu Bridge between China and Hong Kong in the 1980s, carrying huge red, white and blue bags, will never fade. The bags are also known as a *she pi dai*, "snakeskin bag," because of the pattern or the weave. It is so ubiquitous that for me it represents something quintessential about Mainland China. The striped material has even become China hipster-ish, as fashion designers are now incorporating the cloth into their designs and creations.

DAY 12 Motor Rickshaws

You take your life into your own hands almost daily by riding in taxis, buses or, most dangerous of all, rickshaws. Bus drivers are the best; their vehicle takes the most space and vehicles respect them. Taxi drivers smoke in front of their no-smoking sign, slam their brakes and pump their gas pedals, and sometimes stink from sleeping in their cabs, but they do pretty well because of their experience dealing with the mayhem of city traffic. Rickshaws like this one — a motorcycle with a cabin built onto the back — are where you really live on the edge. Rickshaw drivers heed no traffic god but their own will, and go anywhere they like, in any direction, preferably weaving between cars, bikes and pedestrians and against the logical flow of traffic. These tri-shaws have no suspension so you need a kidney realignment after every journey. Battery-powered rickshaws sometimes run out of juice, which means a stop and battery change. The ones in Chengdu lack the aesthetic decoration of those in the rest of Asia, and a crash entails results too dire to contemplate. For some reason hiring a rickshaw is more expensive than hiring a taxi, but they are easier to use for short distances and they have no qualms about packing people in. And if you are brave and able to enjoy the ride, they are in fact really fun — kind of like bungee jumping, just cheaper!

DAY 11 I Rule The World

Cause I'm cute. Cause 20 million of me are born in China every year — that's 38 of adorable me every minute. Cause Grandma or Grandpa takes care of my every need and I hardly ever cry. Cause I get carried around everywhere and I get to eat all kinds of sugary things and there is always someone to make me happy. Cause I don't have any competition. Cause I'm the future and you know it. Gotcha.

DAY 10 The Garbage Collector

This woman and I are probably the same age. That means she was born into a time that rapidly got worse, the early 1960s, when China broke with the Soviet Union and struck out on its own lonesome path. The Starvation Years of 1959-1962, when Sichuan's people produced large amounts of food but had it taken away to feed the rest of China. The Cultural Revolution of 1966-1976, when there was no chance for education and no escape from the countryside for farmers. Things changed in the 1980s. Sichuan became a favored region again because of its connection to Deng Xiao Ping, and open markets flourished. Chunxi Lu pulsated with men standing up in rickshaws hawking fake denim jeans, and women buying Double Happiness brassieres and Moon Rabbit underwear. Chengdu has changed immensely since those days, but somehow this woman's life didn't catch up. She is a recycler, making her livelihood from collecting and selling garbage. My guess is that she came from the countryside but her village or farmland has disappeared in urban development. The political trials are over and there is no starvation, but the grind remains.

DAY 9 High School

These two girls attend the high school close to our apartment. Virtually all students of this age, all over China, wear this uniform, a blue and white sports suit. Since the 1950s, China has educated approximately one-fifth of the world's population, and today education continues to expand rapidly, with new schools constantly being established. Eighty-five percent of the population attends the mandatory nine-year schooling, and nearly all city children go to school. Education is not free, and this means that some children are locked out of education or only attend for a few years. But education is highly valued and parents do almost anything to get their children educated. High school students like these girls attend classes far into the evening, take extra classes in music, art and foreign languages such as English, have tutors if their parents can afford it and study intensely for years to get into a good university. These two girls are students of a famous Chengdu institution: The Number 4 Middle School. Lucky girls.

DAY 8 Tea Eggs

In honor of my dear friend Laura Li, today's posting is about tea eggs, *cha ye dan*. We need more food in this countdown because *chow* (in itself most likely a Chinese loanword from *chao*, to cook or fry) is the stuff that makes this country tick. Tea eggs are street vendor and night market food that you rarely make at home. When travelling, this is a food I often eat because the eggs are always sold at bus or train stations, along with fresh fruit, steamed corn on the cob and hideous greasy sausages of unknown heritage. Tea eggs are boiled eggs that you gently crack and then simmer in a mixture of spices. The cracks in the eggs create a lovely marbled effect and the eggs taste salty with a full-bodied smoky flavor. Recipes vary throughout Asia but most commonly the sauce is made from soy sauce, five-spice powder, black or Pu-erh tea (green tea makes the eggs too bitter). After preparation they are commonly sold like this, in an aluminum cooking pot with a slit spoon to let the sauce drain off. Cost? About 1-2 yuan an egg (20-30 cents). Eggs, in my mind, are incredible objects, aesthetically pleasing with their lovely ovoid shape, smartly self-packaged and crammed with nutrients. They also stand as a universal economic benchmark.

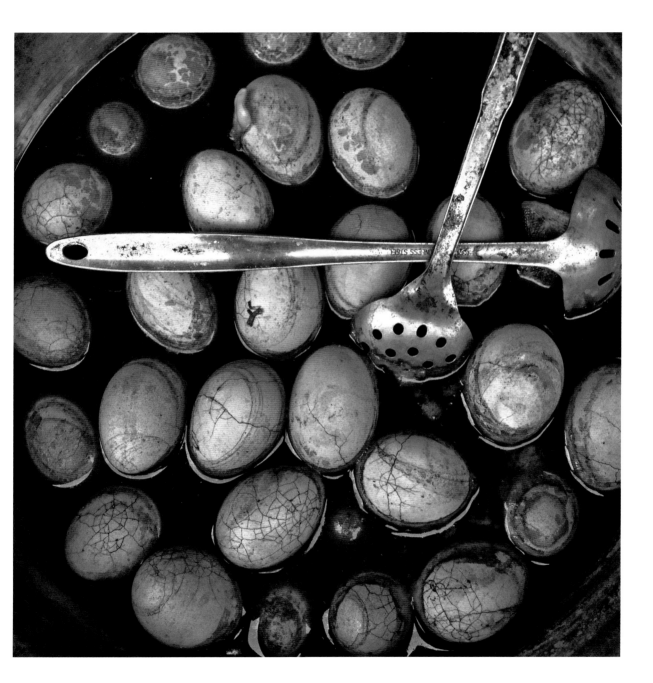

DAY 7 V Is Not for Victory

At what point in modern Chinese history did the grim, stiff, patriotic gaze toward the rising sun photograph give way to the smiley peace symbol glam-grab?

DAY 6 Mrs Li the Seamstress

Mrs Li runs her own business out of a hole-in-the-wall shop inside the grounds of a housing compound two blocks from our apartment. Hers is one of 20 shops that offer every kind of service under heaven: vegetable stand, butcher, egg man, barber, hairdresser (with other services as well), nail polisher, bicycle repairman, odd-shop and jumbly store, locksmith, stationary and school supplies lady, beef rice noodle restaurant, dumpling shop, fresh noodles, and local housing committee. Rain or shine, seven days a week, she is inside her cubicle sewing away. It is cramped but cozy: boiled water thermos, tea canister and tea cup, electric radio, supply cabinet, cutting table, and a Chinese version of a classic Singer sewing machine facing onto the street. She has tattooed eyebrows and the ubiquitous jade bracelet put on when she was young and never taken off. She is tough as nails, gives lots of lip and has pixie eyes like a Chinese version of Shirley Maclaine. Mrs Li hemmed and laid up 10 skirts and trousers for US$15 with a 24-hour turnaround. "*Tekuai*" we joked, like an express train.

DAY 5 How to Clean a Pool in Time for Summer

Self-explanatory. But how sad that the pool will be filled AFTER we move. Last year when the pool was going to be cleaned, the bottom of the almost empty pool was full of koi carp that had wandered in from a side area through a drainage canal when the water was being released. We came home one day to see a bunch of old men with their pants rolled up trying to save the fish with their bare hands and a few empty buckets. I do find it hilarious though that the office staff is cleaning the pool. Pants rolled up, mobile phone at ear, silly little plastic brooms. And a very dirty pool from all the winter pollution.

DAY 4 The A Bridge

I can't get enough of my Chengdu, especially the gritty bits — those fascinate me the most. Luxury shopping malls and glitz leave me cold. How many Maseratis can you own? The drains still stink and the water isn't always hot, even for the rich. Give me a gnarly back street any day. This picture is among my favorites. A small alley leads back to temporary container housing for migrant workers who are building the South Railway Station. Around the bend are the communal showers and latrines. A lonely red lantern hangs sadly from a jerry-rigged TV antenna — a leftover from Chinese New Year and an attempt to make a construction site feel like home away from home. The "A" bridge, with its Jinsha Sunbird gold disc (symbol of Chengdu and Chinese cultural heritage), looms in the background. I'll be travelling under that disc on Saturday evening, heading to the airport to leave. Will I look over my shoulder?

DAY 3 Taxis

When we moved to Chengdu in 2006, the flag-fall was 4.50 renminbi. Today it is 8. Going from 75 cents to US$1.25 is a large inflation for local people, but for a foreigner it is still incredibly cheap. At this cost we take taxis several times a week, and also rickshaws, illegal motorcycles taxis. We ride bikes for anything close to home. Most taxis in Chengdu run on natural gas with large tanks in the trunk. Downside is that in 2006 the traffic was light and pleasant and the pollution manageable. Today Chengdu has the second-fastest-growing car and taxi market in all China, after Beijing. Shanghai is sensible and has placed regulations and high fees on buying new cars, and is desperately trying to limit expansion in its heavily congested megalopolis. Chengdu people, on the other hand, gladly embrace the American attitude of "if you have it, spend it. YOU DESERVE IT!"

DAY 2 Teahouses

The "Crane Call" Teahouse inside People's Park was long one of my favorite teahouses in China. It was the most aesthetically pleasing with a wonderful location beside a lake, my favorite bamboo chairs, good snacks, colorful thermoses and great views from the second floor down onto the people below. I met all kinds of friends here, spent hours reading and writing in journals and taking pictures of locals in various states of relaxation. It supplied part of the foundation of my love for China and Sichuan Province, which is famous for its teahouses. It remains a charming place but much too *renao* — lively — for my tastes nowadays. A foreigner is constantly harassed to get a massage or an ear cleaning. I believe that the name "Crane Call," *heming*, has a Daoist connection to Mount Heming in Dayi, 125 km outside of Chengdu, home to one of the oldest Daoist monasteries in China. Lao Zi, the founder of Daoism, supposedly appeared in Chengdu on the back of a green ram over 2,500 years ago. After Chengdu, he disappeared, never to be seen again.

DAY 1 Exercise Machines

Roundabout 10-15 years ago China decided to get healthy, especially all those pesky old people whom prosperity and stability had created. The government declared that exercise machines should be placed all over the land, and indeed small outdoor fitness stations popped up on every other block like bamboo shoots after a rain. This phenomenon spread all over Asia, and I have even heard that Sweden has installed a few, even though doing anything in public in Sweden is absolutely mortifying for most of us. Day or night in China, from Lhasa to Shanghai, you can see people pumping like crazy on these machines. At the Temple of Heaven park in Beijing you see the most hard-core people, real exhibitionists, doing the most incredible stunts: old grannies hanging from monkey bars for 30 minutes at a go and 90-year-old geezers doing headstands and 100 push-ups. Everyone chatters away at full throttle, giving encouraging *jia you*s — "more gas!" — to all and sundry. You come away fully pumped to get in shape and sign up for the next Long March marathon.

Tomorrow I leave, Good-bye!

DAY 0 Home again

Or? Back on Swedish soil after eight years in China. But it's no longer "home" — that will be the US in a few weeks. When we left Sweden my son was 9 and my daughter 7. Their Swedish was better than their English; now it's the other way around with some Chinese thrown in. These years in China have been among the best in my life. Hope to see you again sometime soon.

First published in 2015 by
Serindia Contemporary
An imprint of Serindia Publications, Inc., Chicago
www.serindiacontemporary.com

ISBN 978-1932476-74-3

Front Cover: Day 92 p. 24
Back Cover: Day 40 p. 130

Designed by Serindia Design Studio
Ingrid Booz Morejohn • Shane Suvikapakornkul
Umaporn Busabok

Printed in China

PUBLISHED WORKS

Kinesiska symboler ©2008 Forma Publishing
På Kinesiskt vis ©2008 Forma Publishing
Resa till Kina ©2006 Forma Publishing

CONTACT

Email: ingridmorejohn@gmail.com
Website: www.ingridboozmorejohn.com
Instagram: ingridmojo
Blog: fivefeetofftheground.blogspot.com
Flickr: www.flickr.com/photos/ingridmojo/